My Gratitude Journal

At the end of each day, Little Garlic always thanked Onion for being his friend and for all the lessons he had learned that day.

Each night before you go to bed, review your day, and bring to your mind anything that happened for which you can be grateful.

There are so many things that we can be grateful for at any time. For example, if we can see, if we can hear, if we can walk, if we can smell, if we can feel, if we can appreciate beauty: these are all amazing gifts. Maybe someone smiled at you and made you happy. Maybe someone shared something with you. Maybe you shared something with someone and made someone happy.

There are so many gifts that we can be grateful for each day.

The sun, the moon, the stars, nature, the air you breathe, and so on. They are all gifts that are yours wherever you are.

And being grateful for each thing or each person in your life is a source of strength that will carry you through the day and give you hope, especially during tough times.

If you remember each night all the gifts that you can be grateful for, tomorrow will be a better day.

It might help you to keep a little notebook by your bed. Each night after you review your day, you can write down whatever you can be grateful for that happened during the day and what you hope for tomorrow.

After you have finished thinking and writing about what you are grateful for, see how it feels in your heart to be grateful. Close your eyes and breathe in that feeling of gratitude from your heart and as you exhale let peace, hope, and love embrace you. Rest in that feeling of goodness and tenderness.

Sweet dreams.

We are grateful for you.

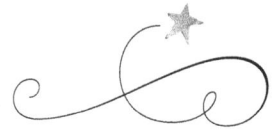

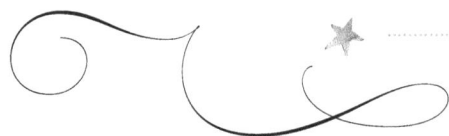

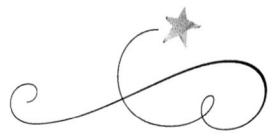

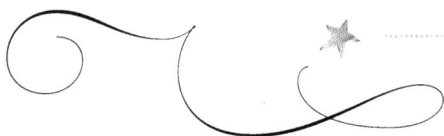

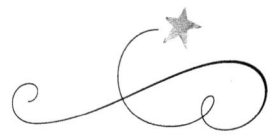

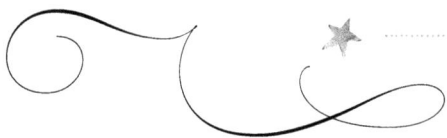

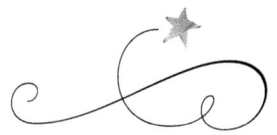

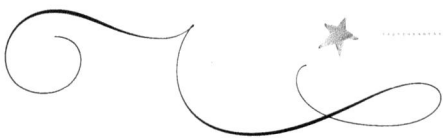

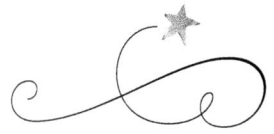

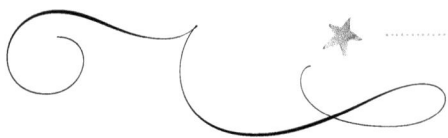

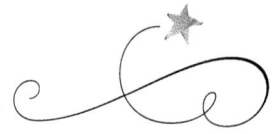

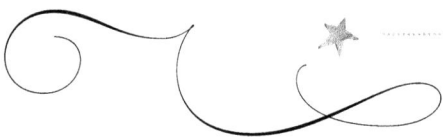

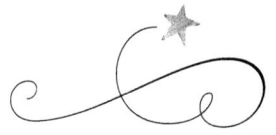

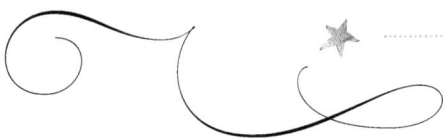

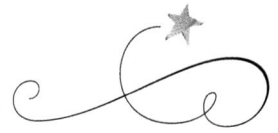

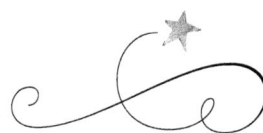

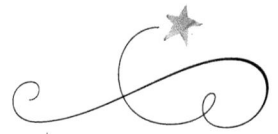

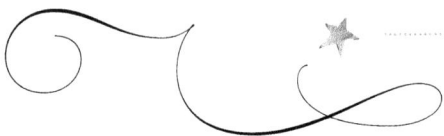

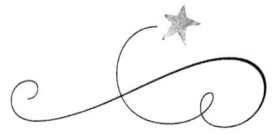

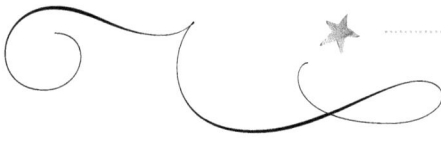

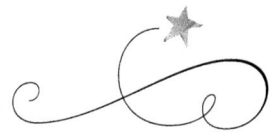

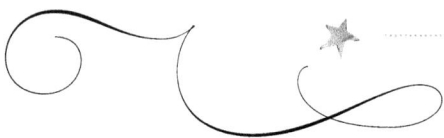

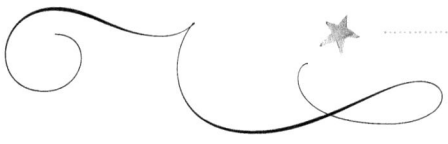

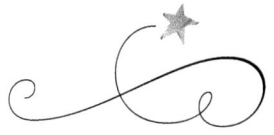

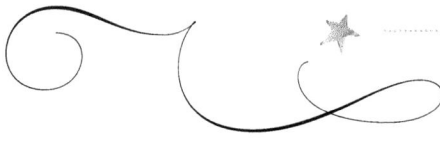

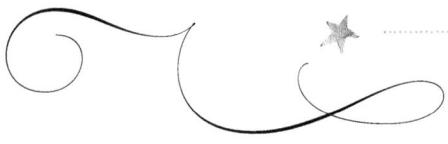

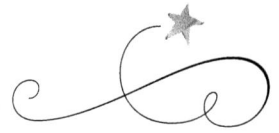

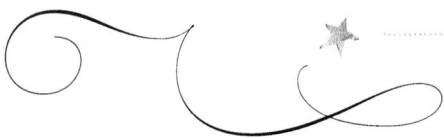

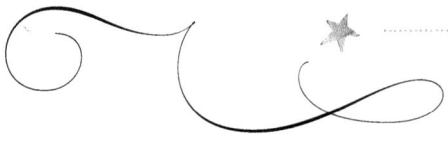

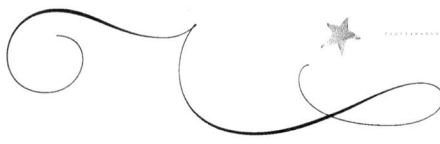

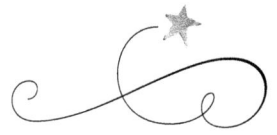

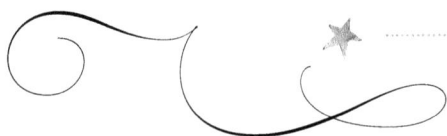

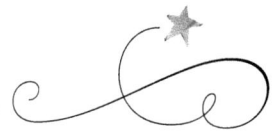

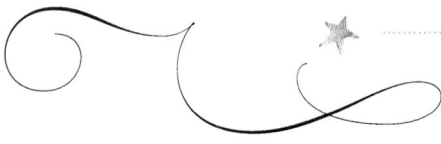

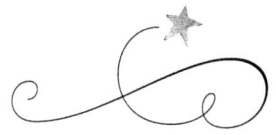

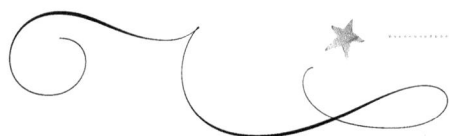

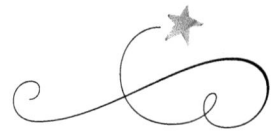

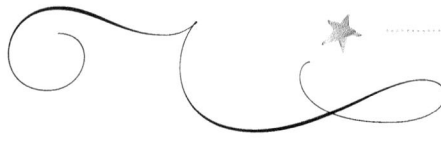

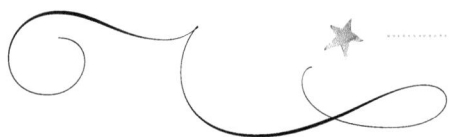

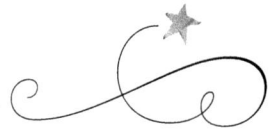

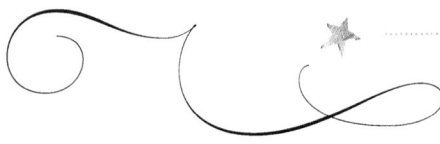

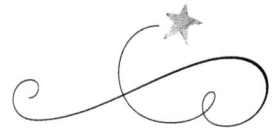

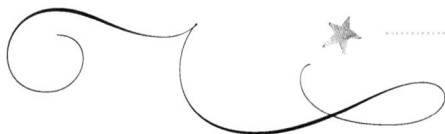

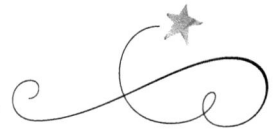

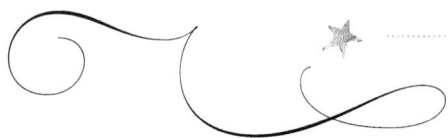

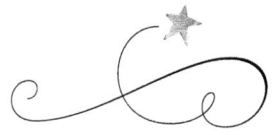

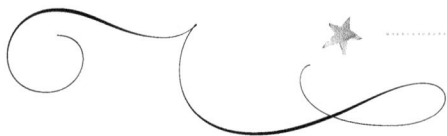

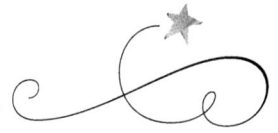

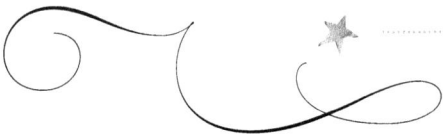

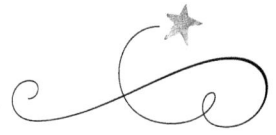

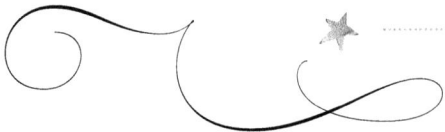

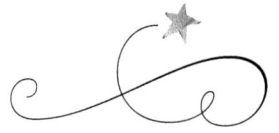

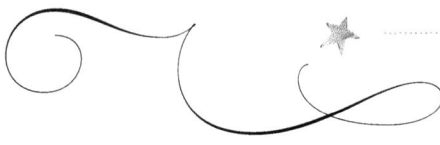

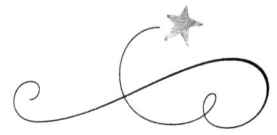

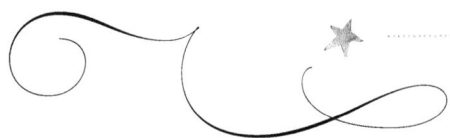

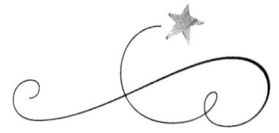

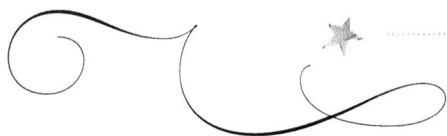

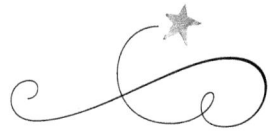

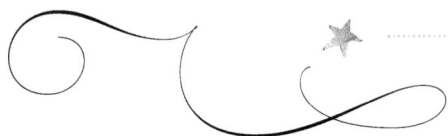

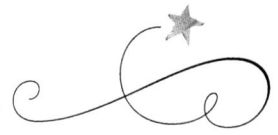

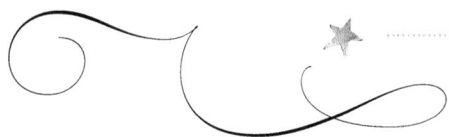

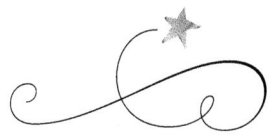

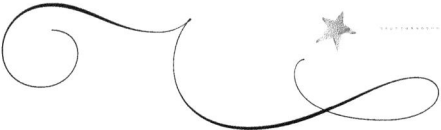

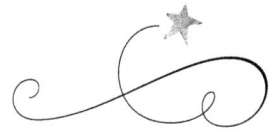

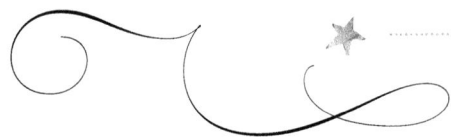

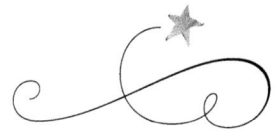

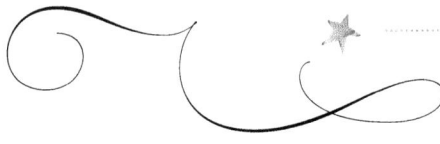

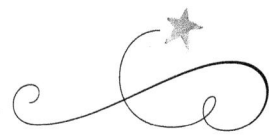

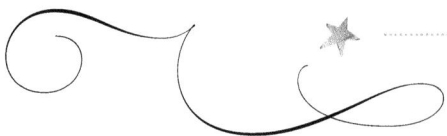

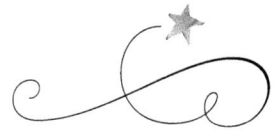

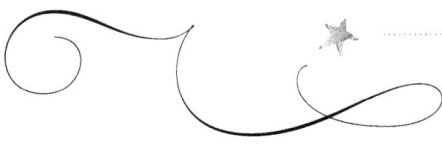

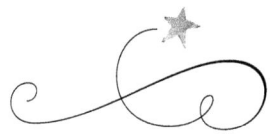

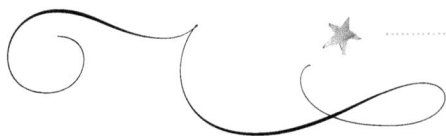

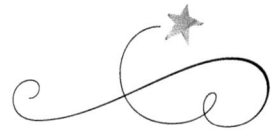

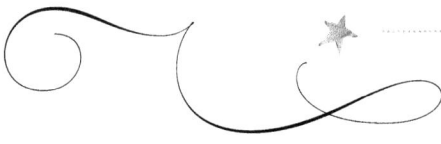

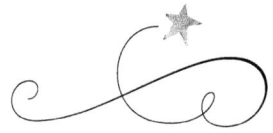

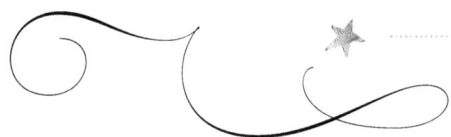

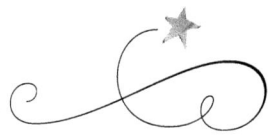

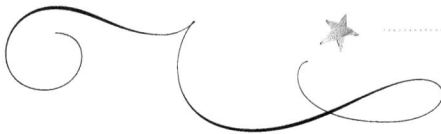

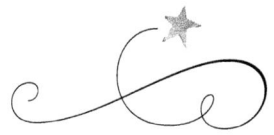

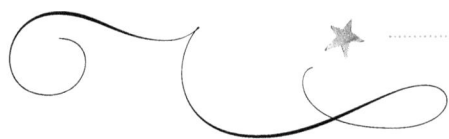

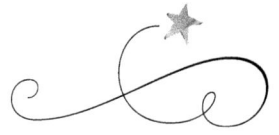

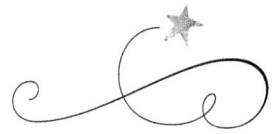

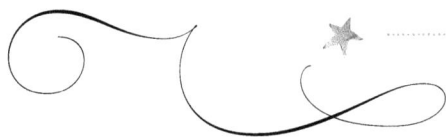

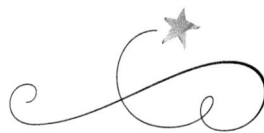

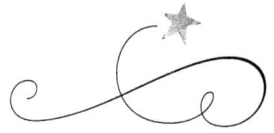

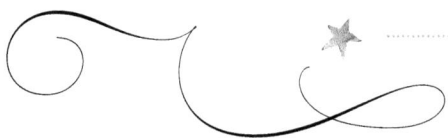

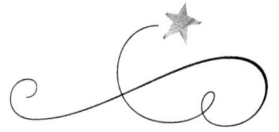

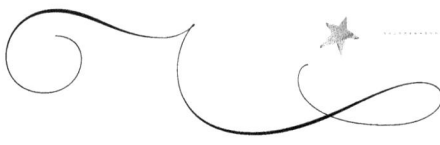

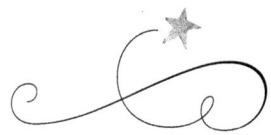

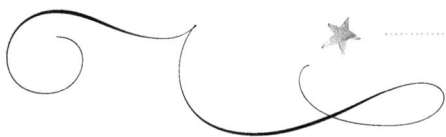

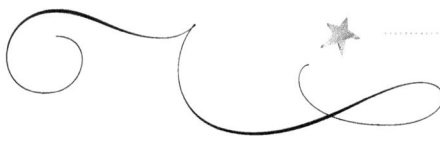

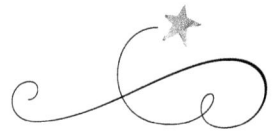

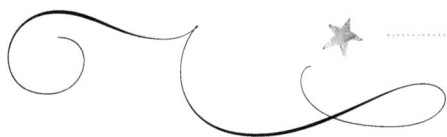

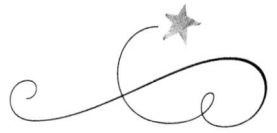

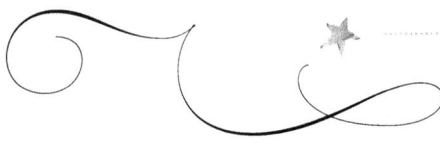

www.ingramcontent.com/pod-product-compliance
Lightning Source LLC
Chambersburg PA
CBHW062334150426
42813CB00078B/2826